Flavors of the World – Poland

From Generation to Generation: Historic Polish Recipes

BY: Nancy Silverman

COPYRIGHT NOTICES

© **2019 Nancy Silverman All Rights Reserved**

Subject to the agreement and permission of the author, this Book, in part or in whole, may not be reproduced in any format. This includes but is not limited to electronically, in print, scanning or photocopying.

The opinions, guidelines and suggestions written here are solely those of the Author and are for information purposes only. Every possible measure has been taken by the Author to ensure accuracy but let the Reader be advised that they assume all risk when following information. The Author does not assume any risk in the case of damages, personally or commercially, in the case of misinterpretation or misunderstanding while following any part of the Book.

My Heartfelt Thanks and A Special Reward for Your Purchase!

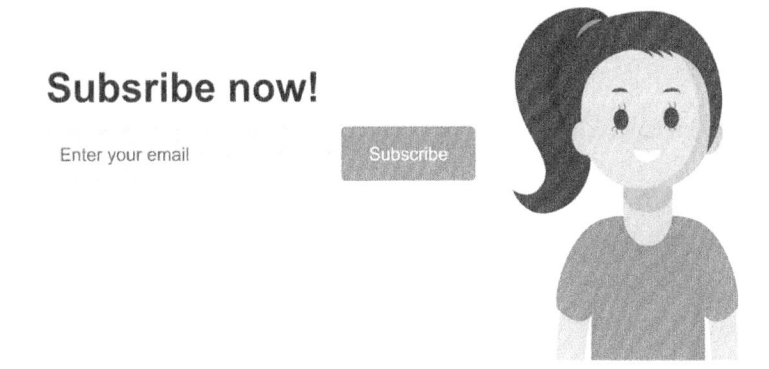

https://nancy.gr8.com

My heartfelt thanks at purchasing my book and I hope you enjoy it! As a special bonus, you will now be eligible to receive books absolutely free on a weekly basis! Get started by entering your email address in the box above to subscribe. A notification will be emailed to you of my free promotions, no purchase necessary! With little effort, you will be eligible for free and discounted books daily. In addition to this amazing gift, a reminder will be sent 1-2 days before the offer expires to remind you not to miss out. Enter now to start enjoying this special offer!

Table of Contents

25 Delicious Polish Recipes 6

   (1)   Classic Beet and Beef Borscht 7

   (2)   Reuben Style Casserole 10

   (3)   Beer Style Sausage 12

   (4)   Polish Style Pickles 14

   (5)   Stew Style Cabbage 16

   (6)   Traditional Cheese Babka 18

   (7)   Polish Style Potatoes and Meat 22

   (8)   Lazy Style Pierogi 24

   (9)   Polish Style Perogies 26

   (10)   Classic Kolaczki 29

   (11)   Savory Sausage and Split Pea Soup 32

   (12)   Polish Style Hunter's Stew 34

   (13)   Tasty Banana and Apple Cupcakes 38

(14)	Sweet Tasting Chocolate Babka	41
(15)	Jam Fill Kolaches	45
(16)	Polish Style Cucumber Salad	47
(17)	Delicious Halushki	49
(18)	Slow Cooker Style Sweet and Sour Kielbasa	51
(19)	Polish Style Dill Pickle Soup	53
(20)	Polish Style Dumplings and Chicken	55
(21)	Polish Style Cabbage Noodles	58
(22)	Delicious Kielbasa and Veggies	60
(23)	Delicious Pierogi Style Casserole	62
(24)	Polish Style Lasagna	65
(25)	Delicious Baked Chicken Reuben	68

About the Author 70

Author's Afterthoughts 72

25 Delicious Polish Recipes

(1) Classic Beet and Beef Borscht

This is a classic Polish recipe that I know you are going to want to serve up whenever you are looking for something on the filling side. It is tangy in taste and creamy, making this the ultimate satisfying dish that you can make.

Serve: 8 Servings

Preparation Time: 4 Hours and 50 Minutes

Ingredient List:

- 1, 1-Inch-Thick Slice of Beef Shank, Bone in Variety
- 3 Quarts of Water, Warm
- 1 Onion, Medium in Size and Finely Chopped
- 1 Cup of Carrots, Fresh and Finely Chopped
- ½ Cup of Celery, Fresh and Finely Chopped
- 1 Bay Leaf, Dried
- 3 Cups of Beets, Peeled and Finely Diced
- 2 Cups of Cabbage, Fresh and Roughly Chopped
- ¼ Cup of Vinegar, White in Color
- Dash of Salt and Pepper, For Taste
- 1 Cup of Sour Cream, For Garnish

- 2 Tablespoon of Dill, Fresh, Roughly Chopped and for Garnish

Instructions:

1. First cook up your beef shank in a large sized soup pot placed over high heat. Cook until is hot brown in color. This should take at least 3 minutes on each side.

2. After this time add in your water, fresh carrots, onion, dried bay leaf and fresh celery.

3. Bring your mixture to a simmer and cook until your meat is tender to the touch. This should take at least 4 hours. After this time strain your mixture and discard the solids.

4. Next combine your broth, beets and cabbage in a large sized soup pot.

5. Cook for the next 30 minutes or until your beets are tender to the touch. Make sure that you stir this mixture occasionally.

6. After this time reduce the heat to low and add in your dash of salt and pepper and vinegar. Stir thoroughly to combine.

7. Remove from heat and serve your dish with a garnish of sour cream and dill. Enjoy.

(2) Reuben Style Casserole

This is one dish that everybody is going to be begging for the recipe. Made with savory layers of Swiss cheese, bread crumbs, corned beef and sauerkraut, this is one filling dish that the entire family is going to love.

Serve: 6 Servings

Preparation Time: 45 Minutes

Ingredient List:

- 6 Slices of Rye Bread, Cut into Small Cubes
- 1, 16 Ounce Can of Sauerkraut, Drained and Rinsed
- 1 Pound of Corned Beef, Deli Sliced Variety and Cut into Thin Strips
- ¾ Cup of Salad Dressing, Russian Style Variety
- 2 Cups of Swiss Cheese, Finely Shredded

Instructions:

1. The first thing that you will want to do is preheat your oven to 400 degrees.

2. While your oven is heating up spread your bread crumbs into the bottom of your baking dish.

3. Spread your sauerkraut over your bread crumbs.

4. Layer your corned beef over the top and top off with your salad dressing poured over everything. Cover with some aluminum foil.

5. Place into your oven to bake for the next 20 minutes.

6. After this time remove your aluminum foil and continue to bake for the next 10 minutes or until your cheese is fully melted.

7. Remove and allow to cool slightly before serving. Enjoy.

(3) Beer Style Sausage

To start things off we are going to start off with some of the most delicious sausage you will probably ever enjoy. For the tastiest results make sure you only use fresh ales, lagers and wheat brews for this dish.

Serve: 4 Servings

Preparation Time: 1 Hour

Ingredient List:

- 1, 12 Ounce Can of Beer, Your Favorite Kind
- 4 Potatoes, Red in Color and Cut into Quarters
- 1 teaspoon of Italian Seasoning, Dried
- Dash of Salt and Pepper, For Taste
- 1, 8-ounce Pack of Carrots, Baby Variety and Fresh
- ½ of an Onion, Yellow in Color and Finely Chopped
- 1 Pound of Sausage, Kielbasa Variety, Smoked and Cut into Small Sized Pieces
- 1 Head of Cabbage, Small in Size and Cut into Quarters

Instructions:

1. First place your beer into a large sized pot and set over medium heat. Bring to a boil.

2. Then layer in your potatoes in the bottom and season with some dried Italian seasoning and dash of salt and pepper.

3. Add a layer of your baby carrots, sausage and head of cabbage.

4. Season with some more dried Italian seasoning and dash of salt and pepper.

5. Reduce the heat to low and cover.

6. Allow to simmer for the next 45 minutes or until your vegetables are tender to the touch.

7. After this time remove from heat and serve while piping hot.

(4) Polish Style Pickles

If you are looking for a festive dish to serve up for your friends and family during the holidays, then this is the perfect dish for you. It is very tasty and shines with festive color. It is guaranteed to get you into the holiday season.

Serve: 25 Servings

Preparation Time: 1 Hour and 20 Minutes

Ingredient List:

- 1, 32 Ounce Jar of Pickles, cut into Spears and Drained
- 2, 8 Ounce Packs of Cream Cheese, Soft and Warm
- 2, 2.5 Ounce Packs of Beef Luncheon Meat, Thinly Sliced

Instructions:

1. The first thing that you will want to do is pat dry your pickles to get rid of the excess moisture.

2. Spread your cream cheese on two slices of your lunch meat.

3. Wrap this meat around your pickle and repeat with your remaining ingredients.

4. Chill your pickles in your fridge until completely chilled.

5. Slice into thick rounds and serve whenever you are ready.

(5) Stew Style Cabbage

A popular Polish cuisine staple is cabbage. With this delicious recipe you can enjoy a classic Polish dish that has been passed down generation to generation. Best of all it can be incredibly healthy for you, making this the perfect dish to enjoy for those looking for something on the healthy side.

Serve: 4 Servings

Preparation Time: 55 Minutes

Ingredient List:

- ¼ Cup of Butter, Soft
- 2 Onions, Finely Chopped
- 1 Stalk of Celery, Finely Chopped
- 2 Cloves of Garlic, Finely Chopped
- 1 Head of Cabbage, Medium in Size and Cut into Small Sized Pieces
- 1, 14.5 Ounce Can of Tomatoes, Stewed Variety and in Liquid
- Dash of Salt and Pepper, For Taste

Instructions:

1. First melt your butter in a large sized saucepan placed over medium heat.

2. Once your butter is melted add in your onions, stalk of celery and chopped garlic. Cook for the next 5 minutes or until completely translucent.

3. Then add in your cabbage and reduce the heat to low.

4. Allow to simmer for the next 15 minutes.

5. Add in tour tomatoes and season with a dash of salt and pepper.

6. Cover and allow to cook for the next 30 to 40 minutes or until your cabbage is tender to the touch.

7. Remove from heat and serve.

(6) Traditional Cheese Babka

This is one Polish dish that is as traditional as it gets. It is usually served up during the Easter holiday and is often enjoyed by even the pickiest of eaters. I know once you get a taste of it yourself, you are going to fall in love with it.

Serve: 12 Servings

Preparation Time: 6 Hours and 40 Minutes

Ingredients for Your Dough:

- 1, .25 Ounce Pack of Yeast, Active and Dry Variety
- Dash of Sugar, White
- ¼ Cup of Water, Warm
- ½ Cup of Butter, Fully Melted
- ¼ Cup of Sugar, White in Color
- 1 ½ teaspoon of Salt, For Taste
- 2 teaspoons of Vanilla, Pure
- ¾ Cup of Milk, Lukewarm
- 3 Eggs, Large in Size
- 4 Cups of Flour, All Purpose Variety and Evenly Divided

Ingredients for Your Filling:

- 1 ½ Cups of Cheese, Farmers Variety
- 1/3 Cup of Sugar, White
- 1 ½ Tablespoon of Sour Cream
- 1 Egg, Large in Size
- 1 teaspoon of Vanilla, Pure
- ½ teaspoon of Lemon Peel, Dried
- 2 Tablespoon of Butter, Fully Melted

Instructions:

1. First sprinkle your yeast and sugar into your water. Stir thoroughly to dissolve and allow to sit for the next 10 minutes or until foamy.

2. Then combine your butter, sugar, salt, vanilla, milk and eggs in a large sized bowl until evenly mixed.

3. Add in one cup of your flour and stir thoroughly to combine.

4. Add in your yeast mixture and beat for at least one minute. Add in your remaining flour and stir again until a dough begins to form.

5. Place your dough onto a lightly floured surface and knead until smooth in consistency.

6. Shape your round into a large sized round and place it into a greased bowl. Cover with some plastic wrap and allow to rise for the next 1 ½ hours.

7. Meanwhile beat together your farmers cheese, sugar, sour cream, egg, vanilla and lemon peel in a medium sized bowl until smooth in consistency. Set your filling aside.

8. Grease a large sized Bundt pan.

9. Turn your dough onto a lightly floured surface and form into a large sized rectangle. Brush your dough with some melted butter and spread your filling over the top.

10. Roll your dough jelly roll style and twist the dough at least 6 to 8 times to form a large rope. Pinch the ends closed and place into your pan.

11. Cover and allow to rise for at least 1 hour.

12. During this time preheat your oven to 350 degrees.

13. Place your dough into your oven to bake for the next 40 to 45 minutes.

14. After this time remove from your oven and allow to cool before inverting it onto a wire rack to cool completely. Slice and serve whenever you are ready.

(7) Polish Style Potatoes and Meat

If you are looking for a filling and delicious dish, then this is the perfect Polish dish for you. It is a Polish classic and is great for those craving authentic Polish cuisine.

Serve: 4 Servings

Preparation Time: 50 Minutes

Ingredient List:

- 4 Potatoes, Peeled and Cut into Small Sized Pieces
- 1 Onion, Finely Chopped
- 2 Bell Peppers, Green in Color and Cut into Small Sized Pieces
- ½ teaspoon of Onion, Powdered Variety
- ½ teaspoon of Garlic, Powdered Variety
- ½ teaspoon of Salt, For Taste
- ¼ teaspoon of Black Pepper
- ¼ Cup of Oil, Vegetable Variety
- 1, 16 Ounce of Sausage, Kielbasa Variety and Cut into Small Sized Pieces

Instructions:

1. The first thing that you will want to do is heat up some olive oil in a large sized skillet placed over medium to high heat.

2. Once your oils is hot enough add in your potatoes and onions. Cook for the next 15 minutes, making sure to stir occasionally.

3. Next reduce the heat to low and add in your bell peppers, powdered onion and garlic and dash of salt and pepper. Stir thoroughly to combine.

4. Cover and cook for the next 5 minutes before stirring in your sausage.

5. Continue cooking for the next 5 minutes or until your onions are caramelized. Remove from heat and serve while still piping hot.

(8) Lazy Style Pierogi

If you are a huge fan of traditional Pierogi but don't want to spend too much time slaving over your stove to make it, then this is the perfect recipe for you. Baked in a rich and buttery sauce, this is the perfect dish to make if you are looking for a way to spoil yourself.

Serve: 8 Servings

Preparation Time: 1 Hour and 30 Minutes

Ingredient List:

- 3 Pounds of Sauerkraut
- 1 Onion, Medium in Size and Finely Chopped
- 1 Pound of Pasta, Rotini Variety and Uncooked
- 1 Pound of Mushroom, Fresh and Finely Chopped
- ½ Pound of Butter, Soft
- 2, 10.75 Ounce Cans of Cream of Mushroom Soup, Condensed Variety

Instructions:

1. First place your sauerkraut and onions into a large sized skillet placed over low to medium heat. Add in enough water to cover and allow to simmer for the next hour or until most of the water evaporates.

2. Then bring a large sized pot of salted water to a boil. Once your water is boiling add in your rotini and cook for the next 8 to 10 minutes or until tender to the touch. Once tender drain and set aside for later use.

3. Next use a medium sized skillet placed over medium heat. Once your skillet is hot enough add in your mushrooms with your butter and cook for the next 5 minutes.

4. Add in your remaining butter, cooked pasta and soup into your mixture. Stir thoroughly to combine.

5. Continue to cook your mixture for the next 15 minutes or until completely heated through.

6. Remove from heat and serve whenever you are ready. Enjoy!

(9) Polish Style Perogies

If you are a huge fan of perogies, then this is the perfect dish for you to make. For the tastiest results I highly recommend serving this dish with some butter, sour cream and bacon to make a dish that is truly delicious.

Serve: 20 Servings

Preparation Time: 2 Hours

Ingredient List:

- 4 ½ Cups of Flour, All Purpose Variety
- 2 teaspoon of Salt, For Taste
- 2 Tablespoon of Butter, Fully Melted
- 2 Cups of Sour Cream
- 2 Eggs, Large in Size
- 1 Egg, Yolk Only and Large in Size
- 2 Tablespoon of Oil, Vegetable Variety
- 8 Potatoes, Baking Variety, Peeled and Cut into Cubes
- 1 Cup of Cheddar Cheese, Finely Shredded
- 2 Tablespoon of Cheese Sauce, Processed Variety
- Dash of Salt and Pepper, For Taste

Instructions:

1. Use a large sized bowl and stir together your salt and flour until thoroughly mixed.

2. Then use a separate mixing bowl and whisk together your eggs and yolk, sour cream, oil and melted butter until thoroughly combined. Stir this mixture into your flour mixture until evenly mixed together. Cover and allow to stand for the next 15 to 20 minutes.

3. Next place your potatoes into a pot and add in enough water to cover your potatoes. Set over medium heat and bring to a boil. Cook until tender to the touch. This should take about 15 minutes.

4. After this time drain your potatoes and mash them thoroughly with your cheese and cheese sauce. Continue cooking until piping hot. Season these potatoes with some salt and pepper and onion flavored salt. Set aside for later use.

5 Separate your dough into two even sized bowl. Roll out on a lightly floured surface until it is thin, though not thin enough to tear. Cut out small circles from your thin dough using a pierogi cutter and brush the edges with some water.

6. Spoon some filling into the center of your pierogi dough and fold over. Crimp with a fork to seal. Place onto a baking sheet and place into your freezer to completely freeze.

7. Next cook up your perogies. To do this bring a large pot of water to a boil. Season with some salt and once boiling add in your perogies and cook until they begin to float to the top. Remove and drain before serving.

(10) Classic Kolaczki

This is a holiday style cooking that is often served up for traditional Polish Christmas celebrations. It is filled with jam, making it the perfect way to satisfy your strongest sweet tooth.

Serve: 24 Servings

Preparation Time: 35 Minutes

Ingredient List:

- 5 Cups of Flour, All Purpose Variety
- 4 Eggs, Yolks Only and Large in Size
- 3 teaspoon of Baker's Style Baking Powder
- 1 Pound of Shortening
- 1 Cup of Milk, Whole
- 4, .25 Ounce Can of Yeast, Active and Dry Variety
- 1 teaspoon of Salt, For Taste
- 1 Cup of Fruit Jam, Your Favorite Kind
- 1/3 Cup of Sugar, Confectioner's Variety and for Serving

Instructions:

1. The first thing that you will want to do is warm your milk to room temperature.

2. Once warm add in your yeast to your milk and stir thoroughly to dissolve. Set aside for later use.

3. Then use a medium sized bowl and add in your flour, baker's style baking powder and dash of salt.

4. Gently cut in your shortening and stir until your mixture is mealy in consistency.

5. Then stir in your egg yolks and your milk mixture. Stir to thoroughly combine. Knead your dough together and place into your fridge to chill overnight.

6. After this time preheat your oven to 350 degrees.

7. Dust a clean and flat surface with some confectioner's sugar. Knead your dough on this surface for a few minutes and then roll out until at least a quarter inch in thickness.

8. Cut out circles from this dough using a cookie cutter.

9. Place a dollop of your jam right in the center of your circle and fold your dough over. Crimp the edges to seal with a fork.

10. Place into your oven to bake for the next 12 to 15 minutes.

11. After this time remove and allow to cool slightly before serving.

(11) Savory Sausage and Split Pea Soup

If you are looking for a savory and filling soup recipe to enjoy, then this is the perfect dish for you to enjoy. It is relatively simple to make and is absolutely delicious. I know you are going to fall in love with it.

Serve: 6 Servings

Preparation Time: 1 Hour and 20 Minutes

Ingredient List:

- 12 Ounce of Split Peas, Dried Variety
- 2, 14 Ounce Cans of Beef Broth
- 16 Ounces of Sausage, Kielbasa Variety
- 1 Cup of Carrots, Finely Chopped
- 1 Onion, Finely Chopped
- 1 Bay Leaf, Dried
- Dash of Salt and Black Pepper, For Taste

Instructions:

1. The first thing that you will want to do is place ¼ of your sausage and half of your beef broth into a blender. Blend on the highest setting until pureed thoroughly.

2. Next place your 1 ½ cans of beef broth into a large sized soup pot placed over medium heat and bring to a boil. Add in your onion and chopped sausage.

3. Then add in your pureed mixture and dried bay leaf. Season with a dash of salt and pepper.

4. Allow to simmer for the next 30 minutes before adding in your carrots. Continue to simmer for the next 10 minutes.

5. After this time add in your split peas and continue cooking until they are soft to the touch.

6. Remove from heat and season with some more salt and pepper before serving.

(12) Polish Style Hunter's Stew

Here is a stew recipe that I know you are going to love immediately. This is a traditional Polish style stew packed full of kielbasa, pork and sauerkraut. This is the perfect dish to make during the cold winter months.

Serve: 10 Servings

Preparation Time: 3 Hours and 45 Minutes

Ingredient List:

- 2 Slices of Bacon, Hickory Smoked Variety and Thick Cut
- 1 Pound of Kielbasa, Sliced into Small Sized Pieces
- 1 Pound of Pork Stew, Cut into Small Sized Cubes
- ¼ Cup of Flour, All Purpose Variety
- 3 Cloves of Garlic, Finely Chopped
- 1 Onion, Medium in Size and Finely Chopped
- 2 Carrots, Fresh and Finely Diced
- 1 ½ Cups of Mushrooms, Fresh and Thinly Sliced
- 4 Cups of Green Cabbage, Fresh
- 1, 16 Ounce Jar of Sauerkraut, Rinsed and Drained
- ¼ Cup of Red Wine, Dried Variety

- 1 Bay Leaf, Dried
- 1 teaspoon of Basil, Dried
- 1 teaspoon of Marjoram, Dried Variety
- 1 Tablespoon of Paprika, Sweet Variety
- ¼ teaspoon of Salt, For Taste
- 1/8 teaspoon of Black Pepper, For Taste
- 1/8 teaspoon of Caraway Seed, Finely Crushed
- Dash of Cayenne Pepper
- ½ Ounce of Mushrooms, Dried Variety
- Dash of Hot Sauce, Bottled Variety
- Dash of Worcestershire Sauce
- 5 Cups of Beef Stock, Homemade Preferable
- 2 Tablespoon of Tomato Paste, Canned Variety
- 1 Cup of Tomatoes, Canned Variety and Finely Diced

Instructions:

1. The first thing that you will want to do is preheat your oven to 350 degrees. While your oven is heating up heat up a large sized pot placed over medium heat. Once your pot is hot enough add in your kielbasa and bacon.

2. Cook until your sausage is lightly brown in color. Once brown remove from your pot and transfer to a large sized casserole dish.

3. Coat your pork cubes with some flour and fry in your bacon drippings placed over medium to high heat. Cook until golden brown in color. Transfer to your casserole dish.

4. Using the same skillet add in your onions, carrots, mushrooms, cabbage and sauerkraut. Reduce the heat to medium and continue to cook until your carrots are tender to the touch. This should take at least 10 minutes. Transfer into your casserole dish.

5. Next deglaze your pan by pouring your red wine into it and loosen the food bits in your pan.

6. Season this liquid with your bay leaf, basil, paprika, dash of salt and pepper, caraway seeds, and cayenne pepper. Cook for an additional minute.

7. Add in your mushrooms, hot sauce, Worcestershire sauce, homemade beef stock, tomatoes and tomato paste. Stir thoroughly to combine.

8. Continue to cook until it begins to boil. Remove from heat and pour into your casserole dish.

9. Cover and place into your oven to bake for the next 2 ½ to 3 hours or until your meat is tender to the touch.

10. Remove and allow to cool slightly before serving. Enjoy.

(13) Tasty Banana and Apple Cupcakes

If you are looking for a delicious treat that will help you to satisfy your sweet tooth, then this is the ultimate treat for you to make. This dish looks just as good as it tastes and I know you won't be able to get enough of it.

Serve: 24 Servings

Preparation Time: 45 Minutes

Ingredient List:

- 2 Cups of Flour, All Purpose Variety
- 1 teaspoon of Baker's Style Baking Soda
- 1 teaspoon of Salt, For Taste
- ½ teaspoon of Cinnamon, Ground Variety
- ½ teaspoon of Nutmeg, Ground Variety
- 2/3 Cup of Shortening
- 1 ¼ Cups of Sugar, White in Color
- 2 Eggs, Large in Size and Beaten
- 1 teaspoon of Vanilla, Pure
- ¼ Cup of Buttermilk, Whole

- 1 Cup of Bananas, Ripe and Mashed
- 2 Apples, Fresh, Peeled, Cored and Finely Shredded

||||||||||||||||||||||||||||||||||||||||||||||||||

Instructions:

1. The first thing that you will want to do is preheat your oven to 375 degrees. While your oven is heating up, grease a cupcake pan with some cooking spray and line with muffin cups. Set aside for later use.

2. Then use a large sized bowl and mix together your flour, baker's style baking soda, dash of salt and ground nutmeg and cinnamon. Set this mixture aside.

3. Next use a separate large sized bowl and cream together your sugar and shortening together until fluffy in consistency.

4. Beat in your eggs with and electric mixture until evenly combined. Add in your whole buttermilk and vanilla and beat again to incorporate.

5. Add in your flour mixture and continue to beat with your mixer until evenly incorporated.

6. Gently fold in your banana and apples until evenly mixed.

7. Fill up each of your muffin cups at least halfway.

8. Place into your oven to bake for the next 20 to 25 minutes or until completely baked through.

9. After this time remove from your oven and allow to cool slightly before serving.

(14) Sweet Tasting Chocolate Babka

If there are any baked breads that are some of the most delicious that you can enjoy, this is just one of them. It is moist and packed full of chocolate, making this the perfect dish to enjoy when you are looking for a melt in your mouth treat.

Serve: 10 Servings

Preparation Time: 3 Hours

Ingredients for Your Dough:

- ¾ Cup of Milk, Whole
- ¼ Cup of Butter, Soft
- 2 Cups of Flour, Bread Variety
- 2 Cups of Flour, All Purpose Variety
- 2 teaspoon of Yeast, Active and Dry Variety
- ¼ Cup of Sugar, White in Color
- ¼ Cup of Water, Warm
- 1 Egg, Large in Size
- ¾ teaspoon of Salt, For Taste

Ingredients for Your Chocolate Filling:

- 5, 1 Ounce Square of Chocolate, Semisweet Variety and Finely Chopped
- 1 ½ teaspoon of Cinnamon, Ground Variety
- 1/3 Cup of Sugar, White in Color
- ¼ Cup of Butter, Chilled

Ingredients for Your Streusel:

- ¼ Cup of Sugar, Confectioner's Variety
- ¼ Cup of Flour, All Purpose Variety
- ¼ Cup of Butter, Fully Chilled
- 1 Egg, Large in Size
- 1 Tablespoon of Water, For Your Glaze

Instructions:

1. First place your milk and your butter into a microwave safe bowl. Heat up in microwave for at least 30 seconds.

2. Then add in your both of your flours, yeast and sugar into your milk and butter mixture along with your water, egg and salt. Stir thoroughly to combine.

3. Next use a stand mixer and mix your dough until smooth to the touch. This should take at least 15 minutes. Cover with some plastic wrap and allow to double in size. This should take at least 1 to 1 ½ hours.

4. Meanwhile make your chocolate filling and streusel. To make your filling mix together all of your filling ingredients in a large sized bowl until evenly combined in a medium sized bowl. Do the same for your streusel and set aside for later use.

5. Once your dough has doubled in size, cut into two equal sized pieces. Shape each piece into a round ball and cover with a damp cloth. Allow to rest for the next 10 minutes.

6. After this time roll out one ball onto a lightly floured surface and form a large sized rectangle.

7. Sprinkle half of your chocolate filling over your rectangle. Roll into a large sized log and crimp the seam. Fold and attach the ends together to form a large sized circle. Place the ring, with the seam side down on a baking sheet lined with some parchment paper. Repeat with your second dough ball.

8. Cut 1 inch slits around your rings.

9. Cover your rings with a few damp towels and allow to double in size. This should take at least 30 minutes.

10. Brush the loaves with some egg wash and sprinkle your streusel over the top.

11. Place into your oven to bake for the next 25 minutes or until dark golden brown in color.

12. Remove and allow to cool slightly before serving.

(15) Jam Fill Kolaches

Here is yet another treat that I know you are going to love, especially if you have a particularly strong sweet tooth. Feel free to serve up this treat as a dessert with a cup of coffee or as a breakfast dish.

Serve: 12 Servings

Preparation Time: 1 Hour

Ingredient List:

- ½ Cup of Butter, Soft
- 3 Ounces of Cream Cheese, Soft
- 1 ¼ Cups of Flour, All Purpose Variety
- ¼ Cup of Jam, Strawberry Variety
- ¼ Cup of Sugar, Confectioner's Variety

Instructions:

1. First beat together your cream cheese and butter in a large sized bowl until fluffy in consistency.

2. Add in your flour slowly and continue to beat until evenly mixed.

3. Next roll out your dough until slightly thick onto a lightly floured surface. Cut your dough into small sized circles.

4. Spoon your jam right into the center of each disks and fold over, making sure to overlap the edges.

5. Place onto a generously greased baking sheet.

6. Place into your oven to bake at 375 degrees for the next 15 minutes.

7. After this time remove from your oven and allow to cool slightly before dusting with your confectioner's sugar.

(16) Polish Style Cucumber Salad

This is a healthy salad dish that you can make for the Christmas holidays. It is cool to enjoy and pretty easy to make, making it perfect for those looking for something a little less complicated.

Serve: 12 Servings

Preparation Time: 45 Minutes

Ingredient List:

- 1 Pound of Cucumbers, Small in Size, Peeled and Thinly Sliced
- Dash of Salt, For Taste
- 1 Bunch of Dill, Roughly Chopped
- 2 ½ Tablespoon of Sour Cream
- 1 teaspoon of Lemon Juice, Fresh
- Dash of Sugar, White in Color
- Dash of Black Pepper, For Taste

Instructions:

1. Place your cucumbers into a medium sized bowl and sprinkle your salt over the top.

2. Allow your cucumbers to stand until they are soft to the touch. This should take at least 5 minutes.

3. After this time squeeze the liquid from your cucumbers and toss out.

4. Add your chopped dill to your cucumbers.

5. Add in your sour cream, fresh lemon juice and sugar in a large sized bowl and toss thoroughly to combine.

6. Season with some black pepper and cover with some plastic wrap.

7. Place into your fridge to chill for the next 30 minutes and serve whenever you are ready. Enjoy.

(17) Delicious Halushki

If you are looking for a traditional polish dish to enjoy, this is as traditional as it gets. Best part about this dish is that it makes enough to feed a large army if need be.

Serve: 8 Servings

Preparation Time: 50 Minutes

Ingredient List:

- 1 ½ Pounds of Pork Chops
- Dash of Garlic, Powdered Variety and for Taste
- Dash of Salt and Pepper, For Taste
- 1 Onion, Large in Size and Finely Chopped
- 1 Head of Cabbage, Large in Size and Cut into Small Sized Pieces
- 1 Pound of Egg Noodles, Large in Size
- 1 Tablespoon of Butter, Soft

Instructions:

1. The first thing that you will want to do is sprinkle your pork chops with a generous amount of powdered garlic and dash of salt and pepper. Place into a large sized skillet and set over medium heat. Cook your pork chops until brown in color. Once cooked remove and set aside for later use.

2. Add in a touch of water to your skillet and mix with the dripping.

3. Place your cabbage into your skillet and allow to cook until soft to the touch.

4. Use a separate large sized skillet and boil your egg noodles in some water until tender to the touch and fully cooked. Once tender to the touch drain your water and add your butter into the noodles.

5. Next chop up your cooked pork chop into small sized pieces.

6. Once your cabbage is fully cooked, add in your pork and cooked noodles. Toss around to mix and serve whenever you are ready.

(18) Slow Cooker Style Sweet and Sour Kielbasa

Here is a great tasting dish for any party that you are hosting. This dish is sweet and tangy in flavor, it is easy to make and one of the best tasting dishes you will make. I know everybody in your party is going to be begging you for the recipes.

Serve: 8 Servings

Preparation Time: 5 Hours and 40 Minutes

Ingredient List:

- 6 Tablespoon of Butter, Soft
- 2 Onions, Large in Size and Thinly Sliced
- 1 Cup of Brown Sugar, Light and Packed
- 1/2, 28 Ounce Bottle of Ketchup, Your Favorite Kind
- 3 Tablespoon of Vinegar, Cider Variety
- 1 ½ teaspoon of Brown Mustard, Spicy Variety
- 1 Tablespoon of Worcestershire Sauce
- 2 teaspoons of Hot Sauce, Your Favorite Kind

- 1 Pound of Kielbasa Sausage, Cut into Small Sized Pieces

Instructions:

1. The first thing that you will want to do is melt some butter in a large sized skillet placed over medium heat. Once your butter is melted add in your onions and cook until tender to the touch.

2. Add in your favorite ketchup, mustard, vinegar, Worcestershire sauce, hot sauce and light brown sugar. Stir thoroughly to combine.

3. Simmer for the next 20 minutes.

4. Place your sausage into your slow cooker with your sauce and onions.

5. Cover and cook on the lowest setting for the next 4 to 5 hours.

6. After this time and serve while piping hot.

(19) Polish Style Dill Pickle Soup

Here is yet another Polish style soup recipe that you will want to make over and over again. For the tastiest results I highly recommend serving with your favorite hamburgers and feel free to serve while chilled.

Serve: 7 Servings

Preparation Time: 1 Hour and 10 Minutes

Ingredient List:

- 1 Pound of Neck Bones, Beef Variety
- 1 Cup of Vegetables, Mixed Variety and Your Favorite Kind
- 2 Cups of Dill Pickles, Finely Diced
- 2 Quarts of Water, Warm
- 2 Cups of Potatoes, Finely Diced
- 3 Tablespoon of Flour, All Purpose Variety
- 1 Cup of Milk, Whole
- Dash of Salt, For Taste

Instructions:

1. Use a large sized pot and add in your neck bones, veggies and pickles. Stir thoroughly to combine and add in your water.

2. Place over medium heat and cook for the next 45 minutes.

3. After this time add in your potatoes and cook for the next 20 minutes or until soft to the touch.

4. Next remove your neck bones and increase the heat to high.

5. Use a small sized bowl and mix together your flour and milk together until evenly mixed. Add to your soup and stir thoroughly to combine.

6. Allow your mixture to come to a boil before removing from heat.

7. Season with a dash of salt and enjoy while still piping hot.

(20) Polish Style Dumplings and Chicken

This is an old family recipe that I know your entire family is going to fall in love. Feel free to modify this dish to fit your taste buds.

Serve: 8 Servings

Preparation Time: 3 Hours and 30 Minutes

Ingredient List:

- 1, 3 Pound Chicken, Whole
- 1 Onion, Medium in Size and Finely Chopped
- 1 Stalk of Celery, With Leaves Attached
- 1 Tablespoon of Poultry Seasoning
- 1 teaspoon of Allspice, Whole
- 1 teaspoon of Basil, Dried
- ½ teaspoon of Salt, For Taste
- 1 teaspoon of Black Pepper, For Taste
- 1 teaspoon of Salt, Seasoning Variety
- 1, 10.75 Ounce Can of Cream of Chicken Soup, Condensed Variety and Optional

Ingredients for your Dumplings:

- 4 Eggs, Large in Size
- 2 Tablespoon of Olive Oil, Extra Virgin Variety
- 1 Tablespoon of Salt, For Taste
- 1 teaspoon of Black Pepper, For Taste
- 2 Cups of Water, Warm
- 4 Cups of Flour, All Purpose Variety

Instructions:

1. Place your chicken, onions and fresh celery into a large sized pot. Fill with some water.

2. Season with your allspice, fresh basil, dash of salt and pepper, seasoning salt, and poultry seasoning.

3. Bring this mixture to a boil before reducing the heat to low. Allow to simmer for the next 2 hours or until your chicken is completely done.

4. After this time remove your chicken from your brother and remove any seasoning. Return your broth back to your pan and add in your chicken soup. Continue to simmer for at least 15 minutes and then set aside to cool completely.

5. Then use a medium sized bowl add in your eggs, oil, dash of salt and pepper with at least 2 cups of water. Slowly add in your flour and stir thoroughly until thick in consistency.

6. Use a large sized spoon and scoop a spoonful of your dough into your broth. Cut into small sized pieces and repeat until all of your dough has been used. Stir thoroughly and allow to simmer while covered for the next 15 minutes.

7. Skin and debone your chicken. Cut into small sized pieces and add back to your broth.

8. Cook until completely hot and serve whenever you are ready.

(21) Polish Style Cabbage Noodles

If you are looking for a last-minute meal to prepare, you can't go wrong with making this dish for yourself. It is mixed with onions and cabbage, making a quick and simple meal to enjoy whenever you are short on time.

Serve: 5 Servings

Preparation Time: 20 Minutes

Ingredient List:

- 1 Head of Cabbage, Medium in Size and Finely Shredded
- 2 Onions, Red in Size and Cut into Thin Strips
- ½ Cup of Butter, Soft
- 1, 16 Ounce Pack of Noodles, Wide Variety and Egg Variety
- Dash of Salt and Pepper, For Taste

Instructions:

1. The first thing that you will want to do is cook your pasta in a large sized pot of water placed over medium heat until tender to the touch.

2. Then heat up your butter in a large sized skillet placed over medium heat. Once the butter is melted add in your cabbage and onions and cook until tender to the touch.

3. Drain your pasta once tender to the touch and add to your cabbage and onion mixture. Toss to thoroughly combine.

4. Season with a dash of salt and pepper before serving.

(22) Delicious Kielbasa and Veggies

This is a dish that is packed full of veggies and Polish style sausage and topped off with some cheese, making this another delicious casserole dish you won't be able to resist. It is incredibly simple; I know you are going to love it.

Serve: 4 Servings

Preparation Time: 1 Hour and 15 Minutes

Ingredient List:

- 1, 10 Ounce Pack of Vegetables, Frozen, Thawed and Mixed Variety
- 4 Potatoes, Small in Size, Peeled and Finely Chopped
- 1, 16 Ounce Pack of Sausage, Polish Variety and Cut into Thin Slices
- ¼ Cup of Butter, Cut into Small Sized Pieces
- 1 Tablespoon of Lemon-Flavored Pepper
- ¼ Cup of Cheddar Cheese, Finely Shredded

Instructions:

1. The first thing that you will want to do is preheat your oven to 375 degrees.

2. Place your mixed veggies into the bottom of a generously greased baking dish.

3. Add in your butter and sausage until evenly mixed over.

4. Season with your lemon pepper and cover with some aluminum foil.

5. Place into your oven to bake for the next 50 minutes.

6. After this time remove your aluminum foil and allow your cheese to melt.

7. Remove and serve while still piping hot.

(23) Delicious Pierogi Style Casserole

If you are a huge fan of pierogies and wish to enjoy something absolutely delicious, this is the perfect dish for you to make. It is a rich and hearty recipe that I know you won't be able to get enough of.

Serve: 8 Servings

Preparation Time: 1 Hour and 30 Minutes

Ingredient List:

- 5 Potatoes, Peeled and Cut into Small Cubes
- ½ Cup of Milk, Whole
- ½ Cup of Butter, Fully Melted
- ½ Pound of Bacon, Finely Diced
- 1 Onion, Large in Size and Finely Chopped
- 6 Cloves of Garlic, Minced
- 1/2, 16 Ounce Pack of Lasagna Noodles
- 2 Cups of Cheddar Cheese, Freshly Shredded
- Dash of Salt and Pepper, For Taste
- 1, 8 Ounce Container of Sour Cream

- 3 Tablespoon of Chives, Fresh and Finely Chopped

|||||||||||||||||||||||||||||||||||||||||||||||||||||

Instructions:

1. The first thing that you will want to do is preheat your oven to 350 degrees.

2. While your oven is heating up place your potatoes into a large sized pot of water placed over high heat. Cook until potatoes at a boil until they are tender to the touch. Once tender remove, drain and mix together with your butter. Mash thoroughly and set aside for later use.

3. Melt your remaining butter in a large sized skillet placed over medium to high heat. Once the butter is melted add in your bacon, onions and chopped garlic and cook for the next 5 to 10 minutes or until your bacon is fully cooked through.

4. Next cook your lasagna noodles according to the directions on the package. Once tender drain and set aside.

5. Then place half of your mashed potatoes into the bottom of a large sized baking dish. Top off with your cheese followed by your lasagna noodles. Repeat with your remaining potatoes, cheese and noodles until completely used.

6. Place your bacon mixture over your noodles and top off with your remaining cheese.

7. Season with a dish of salt and pepper.

8. Place into your oven to bake for the next 30 to 45 minutes or until the cheese is completely melted.

9. Remove and serve with some sour cream and chives and enjoy right away.

(24) Polish Style Lasagna

If you are a huge fan of lasagna and polish cuisine, then this is one dish I know for sure you are going to fall in love with. Packed full of pasta, cream cheese, onions and butter, it is savory and mouthwatering.

Serve: 6 Servings

Preparation Time: 40 Minutes

Ingredient List:

- 9 Lasagna Noodles, Uncooked Variety
- 1 Onion, Large in Size and Thinly Sliced
- ½ Cup of Butter, Soft
- 2 2/3 Cups of Potato Flakes, Dried
- 1, 8 Ounce Pack of Cream Cheese, Soft

Instructions:

1. First preheat your oven to 350 degrees.

2. While your oven is heating up cook up your lasagna noodles according to the directions on the package. Once your noodles are fully cooked, pat dry and keep most with some cooking spray.

3. Then use a large sized skillet to medium heat. Once the skillet is hot enough, cook up your onions in some melted butter for at least 5 minutes.

4. Next prepare your potato flakes according to the directions on the package, but make sure to leave out the mix. Instead add in your cream cheese and stir until evenly mixed.

5. Place your noodles into a large sized baking dish. Spread at least half of your potato mixture over your noodles. Top off with three more noodles along with the other half of your potato mixture. Top off with your noodles and cooked onions.

6. Place into your oven to bake for the next 20 minutes or until bubbly.

7. After this time remove from your oven and allow to cool before serving.

(25) Delicious Baked Chicken Reuben

If you are looking for a delicious meal to make for your entire family, this is one dish you need to try for yourself. It is so good I know even the pickiest of eaters won't be able to complain about it.

Serve: 6 Servings

Preparation Time: 1 Hour and 35 Minutes

Ingredient List:

- 6 Chicken Breasts, Skinless, Boneless and Cut into Halves
- ¼ teaspoon of Salt, For Taste
- 1/8 teaspoon of Black Pepper, For Taste
- 1, 16 Ounce Can of Sauerkraut, Drained and Pressed
- 4 Slices of Cheese, Swiss Variety
- 1 ¼ Cups of Salad Dressing, Thousand Island Variety
- 1 Tablespoon of Parsley, Fresh and Roughly Chopped

Instructions:

1. Preheat your oven to 325 degrees.

2. Then place your chicken into a large sized greased baking dish. Season your chicken with some salt and place.

3. Pour your sauerkraut over the top and layer your cheese slices over your sauerkraut.

4. Pour your dressing over the entire mixture and cover with some aluminum foil.

5. Place into your oven to bake for the next 90 minutes or until your chicken is fully cooked through.

6. After this time remove and garnish with your parsley before serving. Enjoy.

About the Author

Nancy Silverman is an accomplished chef and cookbook author from Essex, Vermont. She attended Essex High School where she graduated with honors then moved on to University of Vermont where she received a degree in Nutrition and Food Sciences. She later attended New England Culinary Institute located close to her home town of Essex, in Montpelier, Vermont.

Nancy met her husband at school in Vermont when the two were set up on a date by a mutual friend. Both shared a love of the culinary arts and it was love at first sight! Nancy and Dennis have been married for 16 years and live on a beautiful property close to Nancy's childhood home in Essex. They have 3 children and 2 golden retrievers named Lucy and Ricky.

Nancy loves growing her own vegetables and herbs in the garden she has cultivated and cared for in the family's spacious backyard. Her greatest joy is cooking in her modern kitchen with her family and creating inspiring and delicious meals. She often says that she has perfected her signature dishes based on her family's critique of each and every one.

Nancy has her own catering company and has also been fortunate enough to be head chef at some of Vermont's most exclusive restaurants. She aspires to open her own restaurant, but for now she is content working from home and building her catering empire with the help of her children. When a friend suggested she share some of her outstanding signature dishes, she decided to add cookbook author to her repertoire of personal achievements. Being a technological savvy woman, she felt the e-book realm would be a better fit and soon she had her first cookbook available online. As of today, Nancy has sold over 1,000 e-books and has shared her culinary experiences and brilliant recipes with people from all over the world! She plans on expanding into self-help books and dietary cookbooks, so stayed tuned!

Author's Afterthoughts

Thank you for making the decision to invest in one of my cookbooks! I cherish all my readers and hope you find joy in preparing these meals as I have.

There are so many books available and I am truly grateful that you decided to buy this one and follow it from beginning to end.

I love hearing from my readers on what they thought of this book and any value they received from reading it. As a personal favor, I would appreciate any feedback you can give in the form of a review on Amazon and please be honest! This kind of support will help others make an informed choice on and will help me tremendously in producing the best quality books possible.

My most heartfelt thanks,

Nancy Silverman

If you're interested in more of my books, be sure to follow my author page on Amazon (can be found on the link Bellow) or scan the QR-Code.

https://www.amazon.com/author/nancy-silverman

Made in the USA
Monee, IL
03 June 2023